SPORTS FOR SPROUTS

Swimming

Tracy Nelson Maurer

ROURKE PUBLISHING

www.rourkepublishing.com

www.rourkepublishing.com

Photo credits: Cover © Wolfgang Steiner; Title Page © Wendy Nero, Crystal Kirk, Leah-Anne Thompson, vnosokin, Gerville Hall, Rob Marmion; Page 3 © Rebecca Abell; Page 4 © Jkha; Page 7 © Kelpfish; Page 8 © Distinctive Images; Page 11 © Purdue9394; Page 12 © Stellajune3700; Page 15 © Augusto Cabral; Page 16 © Rebecca Abell; Page 19 © Axel Drosta; Page 20 © Nick Stubbs; Page 22 © Jkha, Nick Stubbs, Kelpfish; Page 23 © Stellajune3700, Purdue9394, Axel Drosta

Editor: Jeanne Sturm

Cover and page design by Nicola Stratford, Blue Door Publishing

The author gratefully acknowledges Tracy Angelo, WSI, for her swimming expertise and enthusiasm. In memory of Mom, WSI and true lifesaver.

Library of Congress Cataloging-in-Publication Data

Maurer, Tracy, 1965-
Swimming / Tracy Nelson Maurer.
    p. cm. -- (Sports for sprouts)
Includes bibliographical references and index.
ISBN 978-1-61590-236-1 (Hard cover) (alk. paper)
ISBN 978-1-61590-476-1 (Soft cover)
1. Swimming--Juvenile literature. 2. Swimming. I. Title.
GV837.6.M39 2011
797.21--dc22
                                        2010009019

Rourke Publishing
Printed in the United States of America, North Mankato, Minnesota
033010
033010LP

www.rourkepublishing.com - rourke@rourkepublishing.com
Post Office Box 643328 Vero Beach, Florida 32964

We swim in a pool.

We blow **bubbles** in the water.

If we fall into deep water, we should **float** on our backs until help comes.

Our feet flutter like motorboats.

We practice our **strokes.**

Safety first! Always swim with a buddy.

We play Sharks and Minnows. The minnows must swim to the safe zone. The sharks try to tag them.

We jump in.

Swimmers can try other **water sports**, such as snorkeling or surfing.

18

Swimming is good **exercise**. Mostly, it is fun!

Picture Glossary

bubbles (BUB-ulz): Bubbles are tiny bodies of air that show a swimmer is breathing out while under water.

exercise (EK-sur-size): Exercise uses arm and leg movements to help keep a person's body fit and healthy.

float (FLOTE): To float on your back, you must relax in the water and tilt your chin up just a bit.

safety (SAFE-tee): Safety around water means walking around pools, swimming with a buddy, and never using behavior that could risk injury or drowning.

strokes (STROKES): Strokes are the movements you make with your arms that pull you through the water.

water sports (WAT-ur SPORTZ): Water sports use pools, rivers, lakes, and oceans for wet and fun activities.

Index

Websites

www.pbskids.org/itsmylife/body/solosports/
    article4.html
www.kidshealth.org/kid/watch/out/water.html

About the Author

Tracy Nelson Maurer loves to play with her two children and husband in their neighborhood near Minneapolis, Minnesota. She holds an MFA in Writing for Children & Young Adults from Hamline University, and has written more than 70 books for young readers.